W9-CFJ-394

MOLTEN HOT DOG'S
QUIZ QUEST

QUIZ AND ACTIVITY BOOK

GROSSET & DUNLAP
Published by the Penguin Group
Penguin Group (USA) Inc., 375 Hudson Street, New York, New York 10014, USA
Penguin Group (Canada), 90 Eglinton Avenue East, Suite 700,
Toronto, Ontario M4P 2Y3, Canada (a division of Pearson Penguin Canada Inc.)
Penguin Books Ltd, 80 Strand, London WC2R 0RL, England
Penguin Ireland, 25 St Stephen's Green, Dublin 2, Ireland (a division of Penguin Books Ltd)
Penguin Group (Australia), 707 Collins Street, Melbourne, Victoria 3008, Australia
(a division of Pearson Australia Group Pty Ltd)
Penguin Books India Pvt Ltd, 11 Community Centre, Panchsheel Park, New Delhi—110 017, India
Penguin Group (NZ), 67 Apollo Drive, Rosedale, Auckland 0632, New Zealand
(a division of Pearson New Zealand Ltd)
Penguin Books (South Africa), Rosebank Office Park, 181 Jan Smuts Avenue,
Parktown North 2193, South Africa
Penguin China, B7 Jiaming Center, 27 East Third Ring Road North,
Chaoyang District, Beijing 100020, China

Penguin Books Ltd, Registered Offices: 80 Strand, London WC2R 0RL, England

The publisher does not have any control over and does not assume any responsibility for author
or third-party websites or their content.

Written by Cavan Scott

ISBN 978-0-448-47889-0   10 9 8 7 6 5 4 3 2 1

MOLTEN HOT DOG'S
QUIZ QUEST
QUIZ AND ACTIVITY BOOK

Grosset & Dunlap
An Imprint of Penguin Group (USA) Inc.

Contents

Prepare Yourself!

Welcome, young Portal Master. The time has come to embark upon an incredible quest. Do you know the difference between a Chompy and a cyclops? Is your ancient Skylands history up to scratch? Can you remember which Skylander was tricked into donning cursed armor or who got rid of a band of dragon hunters single-handedly?

Above all, how well do you know our enemies?

Turn the page to embark upon your journey, keeping note of your score as you go. Overcome the hurdles ahead and you may just prove yourself ready to take your place among the Portal Master elite.

Good luck.

Master Eon

THE FIRE ELEMENT
Ten burning questions to answer

1 **What kind of creature is Flameslinger?**

A An elf
B A troll
C A fire spirit

2 **When Flameslinger was just a child, he became world-famous. Why?**

A He could fire flames out of his fingertips, toes, and, er, elbows
B He could see visions of faraway places, looking through fires as if they were crystal balls
C His hair was red-hot. You could even cook eggs on it

3 **Sunburn is half dragon, half what?**

A Fire imp   B Phoenix   C Wyvern

4 When he rescued a fire spirit from drowning in a pond, Flameslinger was rewarded with an enchanted bow and magical fire boots. What special power did the boots grant him?

A He would never have smelly socks ever again

B He could rocket into the sky on columns of fire

C He could run at blistering speeds

5 What color is Flameslinger's stylish blindfold?

A Red

B Green

C Blue

6 Sunburn's flamethrower breath can fry the forces of Darkness to a crisp, but what other unique gift does he possess?

A He can teleport from place to place

B He can shoot fiery arrows from his eyes

C He can create burning doubles of himself

7 **Why is Sunburn often hunted by wicked sorcerers and bounty hunters?**

A They want to have him for dinner

B His claws can open any lock in Skylands

C They want to use his feathers in their diabolical potions and spells

8 **What is Sunburn's battle cry?**

A "Roast 'n' Toast!"

B "If You Can't Stand the Heat!"

C "Rise and Shine!"

9 **What was Ignitor's original name when he was a knight?**

A Infernio

B Ignatius

C Brian

10 **How did Ignitor get transformed into a flaming, sword-swinging fire spirit?**

A He was hit by one of Flameslinger's hellfire arrows

B While rescuing a fair maiden, he fell into a bubbling enchanted volcano

C A witch tricked him into putting on a suit of cursed armor

ANSWERS

10	C	5	A
9	B	4	C
8	A	3	B
7	C	2	B
6	A	1	A

MY SCORE

/10

HOT DOG

True or False—show off your sizzling knowledge of the searing Skylander!

1 **Hot Dog was born on top of a volcano.**
TRUE ☐   FALSE ☐

2 **He once burned his nose while chasing his own tail.**
TRUE ☐   FALSE ☐

3 **Hot Dog once ate Master Eon's favorite staff.**
TRUE ☐   FALSE ☐

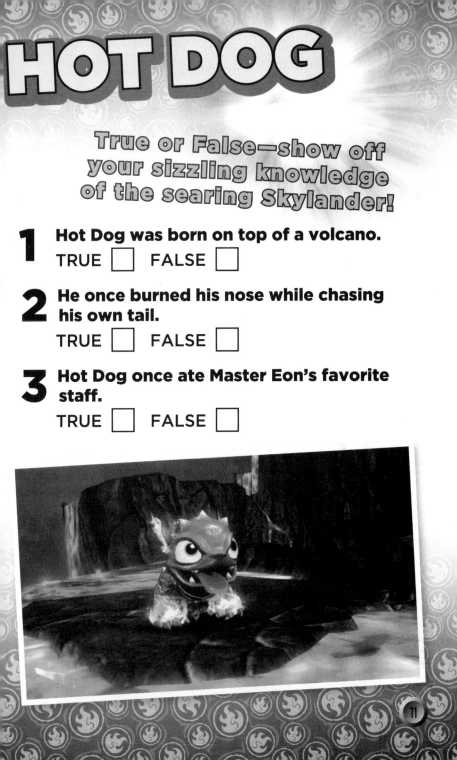

4 He doesn't like helping others.

TRUE ☐ FALSE ☐

 5 Hot Dog can spit fireballs from his mouth.

TRUE ☐ FALSE ☐

 6 His battle cry is "Born to Burp."

TRUE ☐ FALSE ☐

7 If he receives the right upgrade, Hot Dog can flip through the air and crash down like a comet.

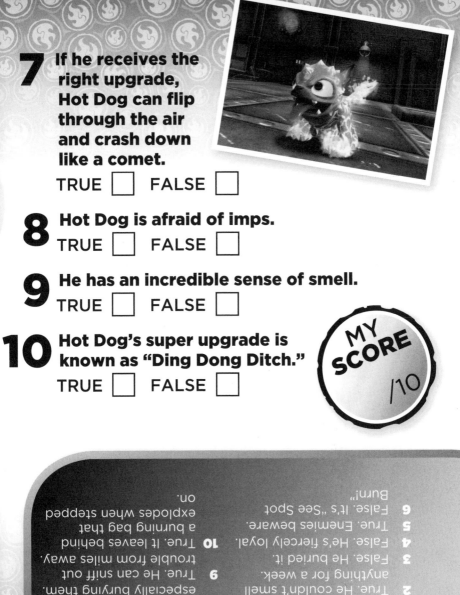

TRUE ☐ FALSE ☐

8 Hot Dog is afraid of imps.
TRUE ☐ FALSE ☐

9 He has an incredible sense of smell.
TRUE ☐ FALSE ☐

10 Hot Dog's super upgrade is known as "Ding Dong Ditch."
TRUE ☐ FALSE ☐

MY SCORE /10

THE UNDEAD ELEMENT

True or False—time to get spooky!

1 **Chop Chop was an Arkeyan wizard.**
TRUE ☐   FALSE ☐

2 **Chop Chop's steel blade is completely indestructible.**
TRUE ☐   FALSE ☐

3 **Chop Chop was discovered in a crumbling crypt by Glumshanks' explorer uncle, Mopeshanks.**
TRUE ☐
FALSE ☐

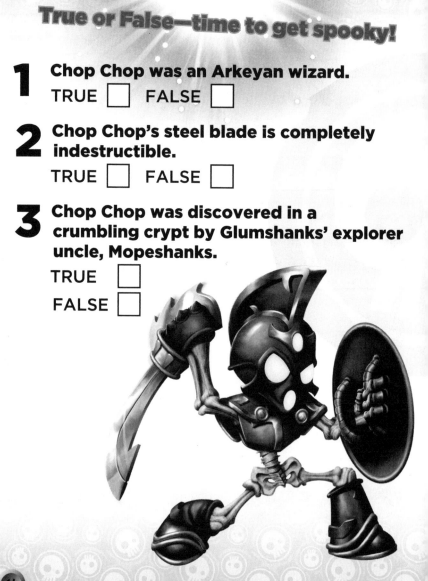

4 Cynder is the daughter of the evil dragon Malefor.

TRUE ☐   FALSE ☐

5 When she was younger, Cynder terrorized the residents of her homeland.

TRUE ☐   FALSE ☐

6 Cynder changed her ways after she was defeated by Hex.

TRUE ☐   FALSE ☐

7 Cynder can summon ghosts from beyond the grave.

TRUE ☐   FALSE ☐

8 Before he was transformed into an Undead demon, Ghost Roaster was a chef.

TRUE ☐   FALSE ☐

9 Master Eon chained Ghost Roaster to a spiked metal ball in punishment for his crimes.

TRUE ☐

FALSE ☐

10 Ghost Roaster's teeth may be pin-sharp, but his skull-like head is surprisingly soft.

TRUE ☐ FALSE ☐

MY **SCORE** /10

ANSWERS

1 False. He was a member of the Arkeyan Elite Guard.

2 True. Those Arkeyans certainly knew how to forge weapons.

3 False. He was found by Master Eon.

4 False. One of Malefor's henchmen stole Cynder from her mother when she was still in her egg.

5 True. But in her heart, she knew it was wrong.

6 False. She was bested by none other than Spyro!

7 True. When she goes into a Shadow Dash, they manifest in her wake.

8 True. His name was Olav and his speciality was sheep-wool stew. Yum!

9 False. It was a spectral ruler who punished Ghost Roaster for eating all his phantom subjects.

10 False. It's a skull-butting battering ram!

Hex

Do you know the secrets of the spooky Skylands sorceress?

1 **What was Hex before she became one of the Undead?**

A   A Mabu

B   An elf

C   A troll

2 **Why did the Undead dragon king Malefor want to capture her?**

A   She was the most powerful sorceress in all of Skylands

B   He fell in love with her

C   She made amazing sheep trotter and cabbage pies

3 **How did Hex first respond to Malefor's plan to kidnap her?**

A   She kidnapped him first

B   She went into hiding with the other wizards, witches, and soothsayers of the realm

C   She asked Eon to send the Skylanders after the dragon king

4 How did she join the leagues of the Undead?

A She asked Kaos to turn her into an Undead sorceress so she could defeat Malefor

B She ate a bowl of Ghost Roaster's ghoulash (made with real ghouls) by mistake

C She descended into the Valley of the Undead to face Malefor and was immediately transformed

5 What happened when she blasted Malefor with her most apocalyptic spell?

A When the smoke cleared, Malefor had been turned into a statue

B When the smoke cleared, she found herself back in her home village

C When the smoke cleared, Malefor was twice his normal size

6 Why are some inhabitants of Skylands still wary of Hex?

A They suspect she has used her sorcery skills for evil purposes

B They suspect she's in league with the sheep

C They suspect she's actually Kaos in disguise

7 **What color is Hex's skin now that she is undead?**

A Gruesome green

B Ghastly red

C Ghostly blue

8 **To protect herself, Hex can conjure up . . .**

A A wall of tombstones

B A wall of bones

C A wall of chains

9 **Which one of the following *isn't* one of Hex's upgrades?**

A Unstable Phantom Orbs

B Caustic Phantom Orbs

C Explosive Phantom Orbs

10 **Hex can summon some pretty weird weather. What rains down when she casts a spell?**

A Skulls

B Toads

C Jellyfish

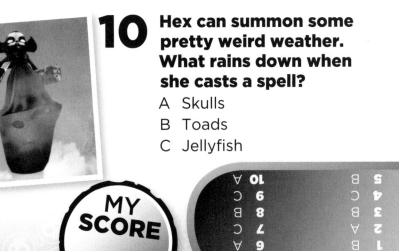

MY SCORE

/10

ANSWERS

1 B
2 A
3 B
4 C
5 B
6 A
7 C
8 B
9 C
10 A

THE AIR ELEMENT

True or False—ten breezy brainbusters

1 **Whirlwind is half dragon, half rhino.**

TRUE ☐ FALSE ☐

2 **Whirlwind can blast rainbow energy from her horn.**

TRUE ☐ FALSE ☐

3 **Whirlwind can control the sea and waves.**

TRUE ☐ FALSE ☐

4 Whirlwind can also heal injured friends.

TRUE ☐ FALSE ☐

5 Whirlwind first introduced Warnado to Master Eon.

TRUE ☐ FALSE ☐

6 Warnado gets dizzy when he spins around.

TRUE ☐ FALSE ☐

7 Warnado can pull his limbs and head inside his shell.

TRUE ☐ FALSE ☐

8 Sonic Boom's scream can knock foes flying.

TRUE ☐

FALSE ☐

MY SCORE /10

9 When an invisible wizard tried to steal Sonic Boom's eggs, she knew he was there because she smelled liver and brussels sprouts.

TRUE ☐
FALSE ☐

10 Once her chicks hatch, they grow to adult size in mere seconds.

TRUE ☐   FALSE ☐

ANSWERS

1 False. She's half dragon, half unicorn.

2 True. The Rainbow of Doom is pretty. Pretty terrifying that is!

3 False. Nope, it's the weather that obeys her commands.

4 True. As long as she's received the Rainbow of Healing.

5 True. She'd spotted the turtle twisting himself through Skylands.

6 False. He gets dizzy when he stands still!

7 True. It keeps him safe during a turtle slam.

8 True. And also friends, if they get in the way. Watch your ears!

9 True. Most wizards can't get enough of the disgusting dish!

10 False. Because of the wizard's curse, they return to their shells seconds after hatching.

22

Lightning Rod

Are you the (h)airy action hero's number one fan?

1 **Complete the sentence: Lightning Rod is a Storm Giant, one of the . . .**

A Oldest races in Skylands

B Newest races to come to Skylands

C Smelliest races in Skylands

2 **Where does Lightning Rod live?**

A The Giant Kingdom

B The Thunder Kingdom

C The Cloud Kingdom

3 **How do Storm Giants spend their spare time?**

A Knitting

B Competing in athletic games

C Sunbathing

4 **What does Lightning Rod wear on his wrists?**

A Giant sweatbands, ideal for mopping up perspiration

B Giant watches, ideal for seeing how long it is until lunchtime

C Giant copper bracelets, ideal for conducting electricity

5 **Lightning Rod was the thousand-meter lightning bolt hurl champion for over two hundred years, until he had a little accident. What was it?**

A He slipped on his cloud and accidentally electrocuted his own beard

B Instead of snatching up a lightning bolt, he grabbed a stray sheep and launched the unfortunate lamb into orbit

C One of his lightning bolts veered into the crowd, blasting an innocent cyclops who was lining up for hot dogs

6 **What tournament was Lightning Rod competing in when he was first spotted by Eon?**

A Four-hundred-ton bench press

B Thousand-meter lightning bolt hurl

C Tiddledywinks

7 **His life changed forever when what appeared in the sky above the Storm Giants' stadium?**

A Kaos's giant floating head

B Occulous

C Malefor the dragon

8 What color is Lightning Rod's magnificent beard?

A Charcoal gray
B Striking gold
C Reddish brown

9 One of Lightning Rod's most impressive tricks is the Cloud Zapper Satellite upgrade. What does it do?

A It teleports you into outer space
B It cleans your cloud so it's shiny and new again
C A protective cloud follows you around, zapping nearby enemies

10 Which of the following is NOT one of Lightning Rod's upgrades?

A Lightning Lancer
B Secret Shockwave
C Electricity City

ANSWERS

1 C
2 A
3 B
4 B
5 C
6 B
7 C
8 C
9 A
10 B

MY SCORE /10

THE MAGIC ELEMENT

Can you conjure up the answers to these questions?

1 **The ancient Arkeyans discovered the glistening oil that flows through all things Magic (even sheep). What is its name?**

A Quickserum

B Quicksilver

C Quick-Drying Cement

2 **Voodood belongs to a brave and magical tribe of orcs, known as . . .**

A The Ooga Warriors

B The Booger Warriors

C The Super-Dooper Warriors

3 **What is Wrecking Ball?**

A A living cannonball

B A mutant blueberry

C A super-size grub

4 Double Trouble wears a mask made of . . .

A Wood
B Concrete
C Bone

5 What is the name of Voodood's legendary weapon?

A The Axe Lever
B The Axe Cleaver
C The Axe Reaver

6 How did Wrecking Ball grow so big?

A He was caught in one of Kaos's spells
B He gobbled up a magic stew
C He didn't. Everything else in Skylands shrank

7 When he was a young spellcaster, Double Trouble ate a rare flower called the Whispering Water Lily. What special power did the plant grant him?

A The power of flight
B The ability to turn invisible
C The ability to create exploding clones

8 **Where did Voodood find his mighty axe?**
A The Cave of Trials
B The Cave of Terrors
C The Cave of Wonders

9 **Voodood's tribe was eventually destroyed by which evil force?**
A Occulous
B Malefor the Undead dragon king
C The Darkness

10 **What is the name of the energy that flows from Double Trouble's staff?**
A Elven
B Eldritch
C Elvis

MY SCORE /10

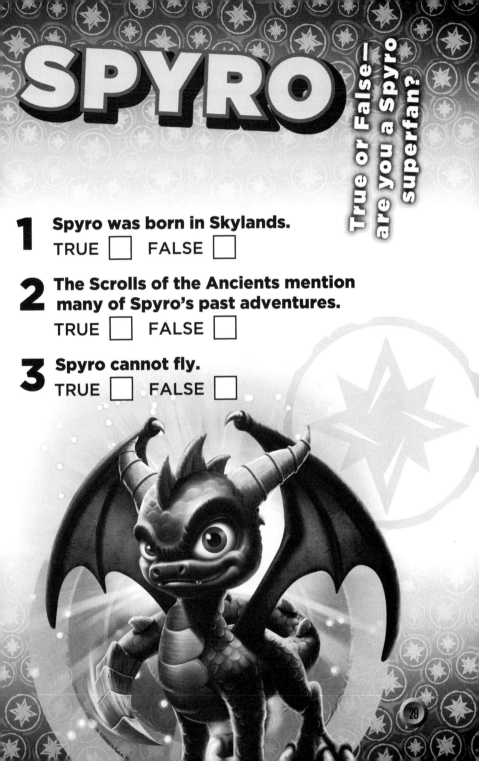

SPYRO

True or False— are you a Spyro superfan?

1 **Spyro was born in Skylands.**
TRUE ☐ FALSE ☐

2 **The Scrolls of the Ancients mention many of Spyro's past adventures.**
TRUE ☐ FALSE ☐

3 **Spyro cannot fly.**
TRUE ☐ FALSE ☐

29

4 When he jumps through a portal, Spyro yells his famous battle cry: "In a Flap!"

TRUE ☐ FALSE ☐

5 Spyro can harness more than just the Magic Element. He's strong in all the other Elements, too.

TRUE ☐ FALSE ☐

6 Spyro freed Drobot from the thrall of the Undead dragon king Malefor.

TRUE ☐ FALSE ☐

7 Spyro can absorb dark Magic and use it against the forces of evil. Oooh, creepy!

TRUE ☐ FALSE ☐

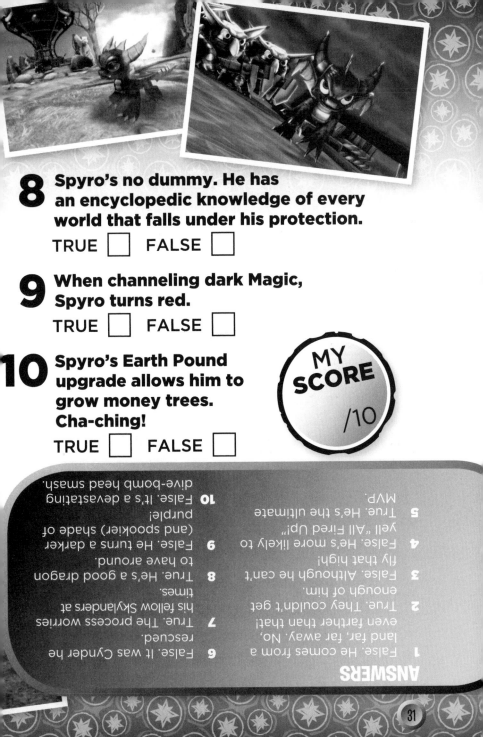

8 Spyro's no dummy. He has an encyclopedic knowledge of every world that falls under his protection.

TRUE ☐   FALSE ☐

9 When channeling dark Magic, Spyro turns red.

TRUE ☐   FALSE ☐

10 Spyro's Earth Pound upgrade allows him to grow money trees. Cha-ching!

TRUE ☐   FALSE ☐

MY SCORE /10

31

THE EARTH ELEMENT

Get to grips with the most down-to-Earth Skylanders around.

1 **Bash is an unusual type of dragon. What is different about him?**
A He is allergic to fire
B He is wingless
C He can turn into a butterfly

2 **How does Bash get around?**
A He hops like a bulky, brawny bunny
B He burrows beneath the ground
C He rolls himself into a rocky ball

3 **How far can Bash swing his tail?**
A 360 degrees
B 180 degrees
C 90 degrees

4 **What is Dino-Rang?**
A A dragon
B An ogre
C A dinosaur

5 When hunters tried to steal his flock, how did Bash rescue his brothers and sisters?

A He disguised himself as a hunter and snuck on board the hunters' ship

B He launched himself through the hull of the hunters' ship like a cannonball

C He grabbed hold of the anchor of the hunters' ship and pulled it back to earth

6 Why does Dino-Rang search for the fabled Twin Diamond Boomerangs?

A He believes they will take him home—wherever that is

B He loves shiny things

C They will give him huge, leathery wings like a pterodactyl

7 Which of the following *isn't* one of Dino-Rang's upgrades?

A Volcanic Glass Boomerangs

B Stellar Boomerangs

C Dancing Boomerangs

8 **Prism Break is a golem, but what kind of golem is he?**

A Rock

B Mustard

C Cardboard

9 **When Prism Break fell asleep in his mine, he was caught in a cave-in. How long was he trapped underground?**

A Fifty years   B One hundred years

C One thousand years

10 **Who found Prism Break in his subterranean prison?**

A Mabu miners

B Troll tunnelers

C Cyclops cavers

ANSWERS

1 B
2 C
3 A
4 C
5 B
6 A
7 B
8 A
9 B
10 A

MY SCORE

/10

TERRAFIN

True or False—just when you thought it was safe to answer more questions . . .

1 Terrafin spent his youth in the Deep Blue Sea.

TRUE ☐ FALSE ☐

2 Before he was a Skylander, he was a pirate.

TRUE ☐ FALSE ☐

3 One fateful day, a mysterious explosion in the sky turned his home into a giant sheet of glass.

TRUE ☐ FALSE ☐

4 After he rescued everyone from the explosion, Terrafin trained to be a seafood chef.

TRUE ☐ FALSE ☐

5 Terrafin can "swim" through the earth.

TRUE ☐ FALSE ☐

6 Terrafin has never won a fight.

TRUE ☐ FALSE ☐

7 Terrafin has orange-and-yellow bumps on his back.

TRUE ☐ FALSE ☐

8 With one of his upgrades, Terrafin gets punchy golden knuckles.

TRUE ☐

FALSE ☐

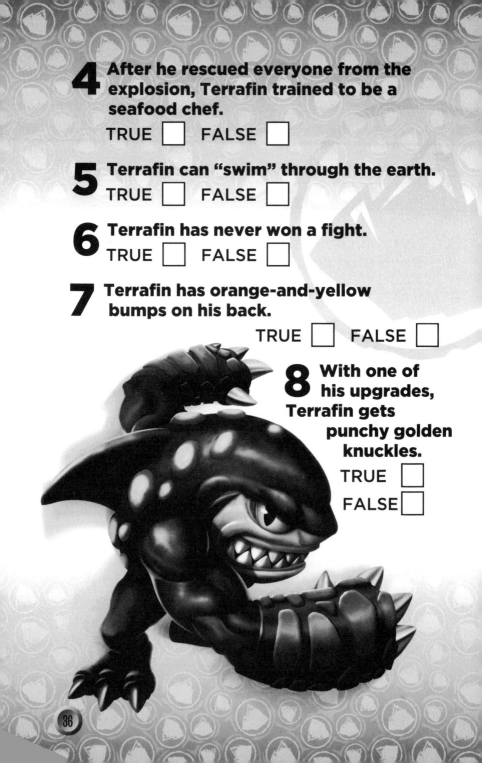

9 Terrafin discovered Drill Sergeant.

TRUE ☐ FALSE ☐

10 When Kaos was banished to the Outlands, he owed Terrafin five dollars.

TRUE ☐ FALSE ☐

MY **SCORE** /10

37

THE TECH ELEMENT

True or False—test yourself on the technology-loving titans.

1 Drobot couldn't fly at all when he was young.

TRUE ☐

FALSE ☐

2 A Tech spell punk created Drobot's robot armor.

TRUE ☐   FALSE ☐

3 Drobot's voice synthesizer gives him a deep, booming voice.

TRUE ☐   FALSE ☐

4 Drill Sergeant was built by the Ancient Benevolents.

TRUE ☐ FALSE ☐

5 Upon his discovery, a grateful Drill Sergeant swore allegiance to the Skylander who found him.

TRUE ☐ FALSE ☐

6 The first order he received from the Skylander was "make me a sandwich!"

TRUE ☐ FALSE ☐

7 Drill Sergeant can fire his drillbits like rockets.

TRUE ☐ FALSE ☐

8 When he was little, Boomer liked to blow up cows.

TRUE ☐ FALSE ☐

9 Boomer was once a member of the troll army.

TRUE ☐

FALSE ☐

10 Boomer can create shuddering shock waves by smashing his gauntlets into the ground.

TRUE ☐   FALSE ☐

MY **SCORE** /10

ANSWERS

1   False. He just wasn't very good at it.
2   False. He built it himself.
3   True. It's even deeper than Lightning Rod's.
4   False. He was built by the Arkeyans.
5   True. And that lucky individual was Terrafin.
6   False. It was "stop things up.
7   True. They become homing missiles.
8   False. He loved to blast sheep (and kind of still does).
9   True. He was an explosives expert ... obviously!
10 True. He really shakes things up.

TRIGGER HAPPY

Set your sights on answering these questions.

1 **What kind of tricky critter is Trigger Happy?**
- A A goblin
- B A gremlin
- C A gorgon

2 **When did Trigger Happy first turn up in Skylands?**
- A When Kaos destroyed the Core of Light
- B When the Arkeyans were banished
- C When a group of bandits were menacing a frontier island town

3 **How did Trigger Happy get rid of the dastardly bandits?**

A He stole their dragon steeds from outside the bank

B He opened fire on them with solid gold coins

C He convinced the townsfolk to form a posse and fight back

4 **What happened to the gold coins that Trigger Happy fired at the bandits?**

A They transformed into sapphire diamonds

B He let the townsfolk keep them, and they became rich overnight

C The bandits swiped 'em

5 **What is Trigger Happy's favorite solution to any problem?**

A Calmly discuss every possible option

B Hide his head in the sand

C Shoot something

6 **How many toes does Trigger Happy have?**
A None   B Six   C Twelve

7 **What else is unusual about Trigger Happy?**
A He's actually allergic to gold
B He has seven toes on each foot
C He has an extraordinarily long tongue

8 **As well as firing golden coin bullets, what can Trigger Happy lob at his targets?**
A Silver coins
B Gold safes
C Gold teeth

9 **What is Trigger Happy's super upgrade called?**
A Infinite Ammo
B Ultimate Ammo
C Unlimited Ammo

10 **How many guns does Trigger Happy carry?**
A One   B Two   C Three

MY SCORE /10

THE LIFE ELEMENT

Ten questions about Skylands' natural heroes

1 What is Zook?
A A Nuttjobian
B A Bambazooker
C A Fast Reeder

2 Why didn't Zook's people ever leave their muddy home?
A Master Eon told them to stay put
B They were all asleep
C They didn't know they could walk

3 Zook's bamboo tube makes a mean bazooka, but what musical instrument can it double as?
A A didgeridoo
B A flute
C An E-flat double bass

4 Which of these *isn't* one of Zook's upgrades?

A Foliage Fungi

B Fightin' Foliage

C Fungal Bloom

5 Which of these statements about Stealth Elf's origins is true?

A She is Stump Smash's daughter

B Her best friend as a child was a prince called Kaos

C She awoke one morning in a hollow tree, with no memory of where she came from

6 Who was Stealth Elf trained by?

A A troll assassin

B A tree ninja

C A squirrel spy

7 Complete the sentence: To confuse enemies, Stealth Elf . . .

A Disguises herself as a green version of Kaos himself

B Transforms herself into a potted plant

C Creates duplicate decoys of herself

8 Where was Camo born?

A In Master Eon's vegetable patch

B By the roots of the Tree of Life

C In a Skylands bamboo forest

9 Camo can create what type of exploding fruit?

A Melons

B Mangoes

C Pomegranates

10 When he's not battling evil, Camo likes to spend his time doing what?

A Carving sweet potatoes and kumquats into comical effigies of Kaos

B Judging the cyclopses' annual novelty vegetable growing competition

C Tending Eon's vegetable garden

MY SCORE /10

46

STUMP SMASH

True or False—do you know a
tree-mendous amount about
the sap-filled Skylander?

1 When Stump Smash snoozes, he can sleep through just about anything. Once, he woke from a nice long nap to find that the forest around him had been cut down.

TRUE ☐   FALSE ☐

2 His family of trees were felled by a team of lumberjack Mabu.

TRUE ☐   FALSE ☐

3 He was so angry that his branches all fell off in fury.

TRUE ☐   FALSE ☐

4 Stump Smash has more than just massive mallet hands to defend himself. He can also spit gob-tastic acorns at his enemies.

TRUE ☐
FALSE ☐

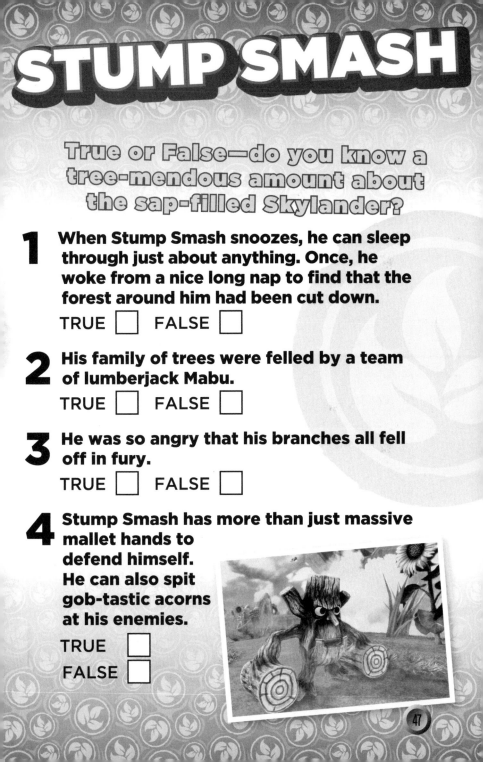

5 Once he had finished pile-driving the fiends who cut down his home, Stump Smash decided to side with that bald bandit, Kaos.

TRUE ☐ FALSE ☐

6 Even though this all happened a long time ago, Stump Smash is still a grumpy guy.

TRUE ☐ FALSE ☐

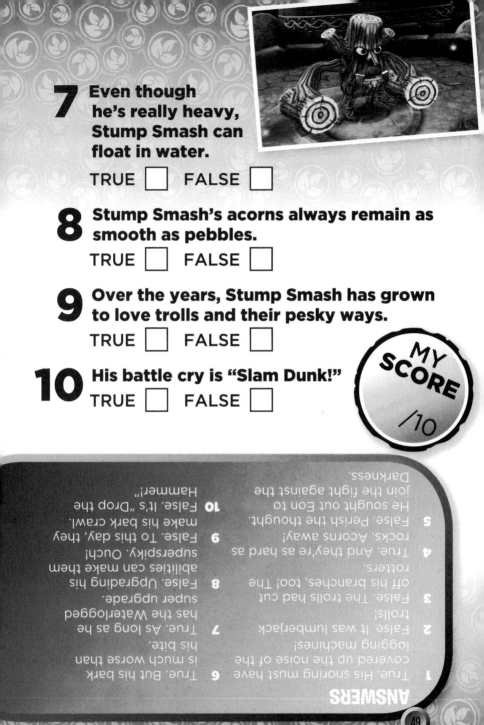

7 Even though he's really heavy, Stump Smash can float in water.

TRUE ☐ FALSE ☐

8 Stump Smash's acorns always remain as smooth as pebbles.

TRUE ☐ FALSE ☐

9 Over the years, Stump Smash has grown to love trolls and their pesky ways.

TRUE ☐ FALSE ☐

10 His battle cry is "Slam Dunk!"

TRUE ☐ FALSE ☐

MY SCORE /10

ANSWERS

1 True. His snoring must have covered up the noise of the logging machines!

2 False. It was lumberjack trolls!

3 False. The trolls had cut off his branches, too! The rotters.

4 True. And they're as hard as rocks. Acorns away!

5 False. Perish the thought. He sought out Eon to join the fight against the Darkness.

6 True. But his bark is much worse than his bite.

7 True. As long as he has the Waterlogged super upgrade.

8 False. Upgrading his abilities can make them superspiky. Ouch!

9 False. To this day, they make his bark crawl.

10 False. It's "Drop the Hammer!"

49

THE WATER ELEMENT

True or False—dive into these aquatic quandaries.

1 **Slam Bam is an ice ogre.**

TRUE ☐   FALSE ☐

2 **Kaos destroyed Slam Bam's floating iceberg just because the Skylander made better sandwiches than him.**

TRUE ☐   FALSE ☐

3 **Slam Bam has six frosty arms.**

TRUE ☐   FALSE ☐

4 Wham-Shell, the crusading crustacean, is a royal prince.

TRUE ☐   FALSE ☐

5 Wham-Shell hates trolls because they invaded his underwater kingdom to drill for oil.

TRUE ☐

FALSE ☐

6 Wham-Shell's Malacostracan Mace fires seahorse missiles.

TRUE ☐   FALSE ☐

7 Zap is a water dragon who was raised by a family of electric eels.

TRUE ☐

FALSE ☐

MY
SCORE
/10

8 Zap was given a special electrified golden crown that is always fully charged to give bad guys a shock!

TRUE ☐

FALSE ☐

9 Zap can slide into battle on slippery sea slime.

TRUE ☐   FALSE ☐

10 The two-legged sea creatures that live on beaches and will try to cut off your ankles with their sawlike bills are called saw ducks.

TRUE ☐   FALSE ☐

Gill Grunt

1 **Gill Grunt is a . . .**
A Fishman
B Gillman
C Finman

It's time for Gill Power!

2 **Which of the following *isn't* one of Gill's battle cries?**

A "Fins of Fury!"
B "Follow the Freak!"
C "Fear the Fish!"

3 When he was younger, Gill fell head over fins in love with a beautiful girl. Ahhhhh. But what kind of girl was she?

A   A sharkwoman
B   A squidlass
C   A mermaid

4 Where did Gill meet his girlfriend?

A   A misty lagoon
B   A smelly swamp
C   A choppy lake

5 Which of the following is one of Gill's power upgrades?

A   Whirlpool Cannon
B   Anchor Cannon
C   Octopus Cannon

6 Who kidnapped Gill's girlfriend?

A   Kaos
B   Trolls
C   Pirates

7 Gill was sent by Master Eon to ask which watery warrior to become a Skylander?

A Wham-Shell
B Slam Bam
C Zap

8 Which of these upgrades allows Gill to fly?

A Fishy Flight
B Thruster Flight
C Booster Flight

9 How many prongs do Gill's Quadent Harpoons have?

A Two
B Three
C Four

10 What happens to the starfish that Gill fires out of his Neptune Gun?

A They explode
B They grow to huge proportions
C They eat anything in their path

ANSWERS

1 B
2 B
3 C
4 A
5 B
6 C
7 A
8 B
9 C
10 A

MY SCORE /10

WHICH SKYLANDER ARE YOU?

Your quest is almost over, so why not take a break to find out which Skylander you are most like?

 1 Which is your favorite element?

A Magic

B Water

C Tech

D Fire

E Life

F Undead

G Air

H Earth

2 What kind of food do you prefer?

A A bit of everything
B Seafood
C Mexican
D Anything hot and spicy
E Vegetables
F Ghosts
G Meat, and lots of it
H Rock candy

3 What kind of party would you most like to be invited to?

A I don't care as long as my friends are there
B A pool party
C Paintball
D A beach party
E A hide-and-seek championship
F I don't care as long as there's loads to eat
G One with lots of games
H I don't like parties. Too many people

4 Which of the following best describes your personality?

A Fearless
B Loyal
C Manic
D Brave
E Sneaky
F Creepy
G Heroic
H Solitary

5 Which of these skills would you most like to learn?

A How to fly
B Fishing
C Shooting
D Having a nose for danger
E Tracking
F Cooking
G Learn skills? I'm pretty perfect already!
H Rock climbing

6 Where do you like to go on vacation?

A Anywhere as long as we fly there

B By the sea

C The Wild West

D Anywhere hot

E A nice green place

F Somewhere where there isn't much sun

G Somewhere sunny so I can show off my muscles

H Somewhere where there are no crowds

7 What kind of movies do you like?

A Superhero films

B Romance

C Westerns

D Action movies

E Spy movies

F Scary films

G Sports films

H Silent movies. I don't like noise

8 What are you like when working in a team?

A I'm a natural leader

B I look after my teammates

C I'm eager to hit the target

D I'll always protect my friends

E I keep quiet and get the job done

F People are sometimes a little scared of me

G I'm happy to help. After all, I'm good—really good

H I'd rather work alone, but I'll play my part

You are like:

Mostly As: Spyro
You're courageous and strong-willed; a natural leader and a born hero.

Mostly Bs: Gill Grunt
You have a big heart and are always ready to protect your friends.

Mostly Cs: Trigger Happy
You're fast, furious, and quick to jump into action. You're one wild guy!

Mostly Ds: Molten Hot Dog
You need to keep your fireballs in check, but are loyal and brave.

Mostly Es: Stealth Elf
Quick and dependable, everyone wants you on their team.

Mostly Fs: Ghost Roaster
You have a dark side, but you fight for what's right. Oh, and you like your food!

Mostly Gs: Lightning Rod
You're always the best at what you do— and you know it.

Mostly Hs: Prism Break
You like your own company, but you can always be relied on.

FINAL SCORE

MY TOTAL

Time to add up those scores, young Portal Master. Write your grand total here and see how well you did.

0–10: Not that powerful . . . yet!
Hmmm. I'm not sure you've been paying attention. I'll get Hugo to dig out some Skylands history books for you. Don't worry—we all had to start somewhere.

11–25: Showing Portal Promise!
You're on the road to becoming a legendary Portal Master. Keep practicing and you'll soon be named among the greats, like, er, me.

26–75: One to Watch!
Well done, that's a good effort. Get to know your Skylanders a bit better and you'll soon be a real force to reckon with.

76–149: Super Skylands Skills!
Impressive. You're almost as knowledgeable as me—although I think my beard is better. Either way, Kaos had better watch out.

150+: Portal Master Supreme!

Congratulations—what an amazing score!
Skylands is in safe hands. Darkness will
never fall while you are a Portal Master.

Master Eon

SKYLANDERS SPYRO'S ADVENTURE

Master Eon's

Bonus
giant poster!

OFFICIAL GUIDE

THE **MACHINE** OF **DOOM**

THE MASK OF POWER **SPYRO** VERSUS THE MEGA MONSTERS

BATTLE FOR SKYLANDS

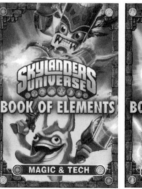

BOOK OF ELEMENTS

MAGIC & TECH

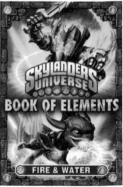

BOOK OF ELEMENTS

FIRE & WATER